I FELL IN LOVE WITH THE SON OF A WITCH

by
Saffron
MindBenders Collections
Deborah Stevens

TABLE OF CONTENT

DEDICATION

I dedicate this masterpiece to my wonderful children, Ebonee (Nieko) "Londyn" Tony, and Ronnie along with my Glambaby Melrose (Mellie).

I love you all.

ACKNOWLEDGMENTS

I want to thank my Lord and Savior, Jesus Christ, for giving me peace that surpasses all understanding.

To my spiritual Father in the Gospel, Bishop Vance R. Oldes; author of From Cocaine to Collar, for leading and guiding me to all truths through the word of God, and for his transparency.

Also, I appreciate the 1st Lady, Nicole Oldes, for being the epitome of a True Lady.

Special acknowledgment to my daughter by another mother, Lanetta Grant, Author of Beauty after Broken for inspiring and encouraging me to finish this book.

Also, I appreciate; my support team- my besties, Apostle Marthetta Gamble, Deborah (Deb) Washington, and Barbra Lucus.

I love you all.

Debbie (Saffron) can be reached by email: alleyesonbiz@gmail.com

FORWARD

There are certain character traits to look out for in a person you're considering going into a relationship with. There are a lot of people who ignore this and then find themselves committing time and emotions to people they'd end up regretting for the rest of their lives. Checking helps you to know the underlying causes of certain actions, what to expect, and the things you can tolerate going forward. That being said, this book, I FELL IN LOVE WITH THE SON OF A WITCH is creative about a beautiful young lady in her early twenties who ignored the red flags she should have questioned or taken note of, but ended up abused not only by her boyfriend but also his manipulative mother. It'd be a great read for young people, especially ladies, as they'd be able to understand better why it is important to watch out for people who act in extreme or dysfunctional ways and probably offer help where necessary.

PROLOGUE

It was a beautiful Wednesday evening; just before sunset, Stacy headed to the store to get some supplies. It had been such a stressful day at work, but she needed to restock her house. She just couldn't procrastinate anymore. She'd usually go shopping with her friends from the office but they kept bailing out on her, she just had to go do it all herself. Her favorite place to shop was quite a distance from her office, so taking a taxi there was inevitable.

Fifteen minutes beside the road, just outside her office, she was still standing, waiting to get a taxi.

"I need to save up for a new car", Stacy thought to herself as she watched people drive by. Just then, a taxi pulled over.

"Going somewhere?" The taxi man asked, winking almost way out of proportion for the simple question.

Yes, sure. There's a store that's a few kilometres from here and I need to get there before they close for the day.

"Get in then", The taxi driver said, throwing his arm in the air, in a way that signaled Stacy in. She got in and the taxi driver sped off; a speed commensurate, and perhaps exceeding Stacy's reason for hopping in.

Music played from the car radio and occasionally, she nodded to the beat of the song.

"You can drop me right here. This is where I'll alight".

She brought out her purse, counted some money with extra change and gave to the man. He stretched out his hand and took the money from her with a warm smile on his face.

"He's nice", she thought as she walked into the store. Head down, eyes on her phone, sending and replying messages, giggling occasionally as she took slow steps into the building which was moderately large.

In her early twenties, Stacy was an attractive young lady with a curvy shape, beautiful skin (body to die for) and had a distinctive carriage style. She wore this killer blue dress, tight and fitted in all the right places with black heels to match. Her hair; dark with curls and fell gloriously behind her.

Marco had a though fleeting, but just enough sight of her stepping out of the taxi, he couldn't take his eyes off, her beauty was captivating and he suddenly felt this urge to walk up to her and say something... anything at all.

As she stepped out the store, holding shopping bags with both hands, he excused his friend and walked up to her.

"Hello there...."

Stacy turned to see who it was, talking to her.

Oh my! he's fine! You know, Ice Cube, Gerald Levert fine or some would say Ghost from Power, Barack Obama or maybe even Irdris Alba fine! (You get the picture)....

How're you doing? You're really beautiful, I can't help but notice that. Can I get your number so I can call you and... you know, go on a date maybe...? I'm Marco by the way, nice to meet you."

"Stacy...." She said stretching out her hand for his phone.

Usually, she'd put on her defences for guys who approached her but this one looked decent and responsible. He was polite too. It wouldn't cost anything to give him her phone number at least.

She typed her digits quickly and handed the phone back to him. Her smile was infectious, she was unbelievable.

"Okay, expect my call, Marco said smiling".

This was going to be an encounter that would take her through the craziest experience of her life and if someone had told her that, she'd pray she never gets to meet anyone like him.

Not even an hour had gone by, yet, he called her phone. This time, she was already back home trying to whip something up for herself for dinner.

Stacy loved to cook, she prepared her meals most times and rarely ate out. She had a lot of recipes off hand. Good thing she spent most of her life around her grandma. Wiping her hands with a clean kitchen rag, she picked up the phone which was on a table right beside her.

Seeing the strange number, she knew this had to be the guy she had just met at the store.

"Hello.....?" She said with a subtle voice.

And yes, the journey begins, it's sure going to be a bumpy ride. Hold on tight, fasten your seat belts. Let's go!

CHAPTER ONE

HEAD OVER HILLS

Marco and Stacy talked on the phone, all day, every day. They talked while she was in the shower, in the kitchen, in bed, at work, just anywhere at all. He was consistent in his push to win her over, and so it went from bringing her bouquets of flowers, gifts, handing her treats, to expensive dinner dates and sometimes lunch breaks. Whatever it took, he went all out to make it happen for her. The man knew what he wanted and didn't stop till he got it.

Stacy was completely blown away by his tenderness. Such a man can only exist in a fairytale; this was probably her own fairytale. It seemed too good to be true. Alas, it was true, and she couldn't deny that she had begun to develop feelings for Marco. You know, wanting to spend time talking to him, being with him and just hearing him say all the nice things that made her drown in the pool of emotions.

One evening, they stepped out together. Marco was interested in showing her a new restaurant he'd just discovered.

They had great food and offered awesome services. While they sat, a waiter came around to take their orders and complimented Stacy. She looked really gorgeous being who she was; she was never wrong when it came to fashion.

Marco was offended at the comment of the waiter and asked him to do no such thing anymore. At first, Stacy thought he was joking about the situation, but when he kept going on about it, she realized he was really mad. It bothered her why he'd taken the harmless comment of the waiter so much to heart.

So many other times, there were incidences where he'd act extremely jealous and possessive of her. He didn't like that she had any form of communication whatsoever with male folks, even with her colleagues at the office.

Such behavior was totally abnormal and enough reason for Stacy to think thoroughly if she could handle a guy who seemed a little bit too controlling. She felt uneasy most times when it happened, but she'd never had a close experience and thought she was overreacting.

Are you still holding on tight?

Great, we're down to the aspect of coition (the time for lovemaking, you know).

Marco had plans for this day the very moment he set his

eyes on Stacy. He really couldn't wait to have her in bed but had to be patient with the wooing process. It was not his first time; he had become really good at making a woman fall for him, and somehow it was always easy for him.

The day it happened, he had to make it really special, create an atmosphere that she wouldn't be able to resist. He invited her to spend the night with him at a hotel. That evening, he went over to her place to pick her up after work; she looked stunning as usual, and with what she wore, it was almost like she knew what was going down tonight.

He had all her favorite things at her disposal, from chocolates to strawberries, to lobster dinner, to her favorite wine, and of course, a bouquet of rose flowers. The room was lit with colorful lights and had a really captivating fragrance.

Romantic music played in the background, going from Gerald Lavert, Sade, Luther Tyrese, Anita Baker, Mary J, Stevie Issa, Jeneko Aiko, Toni Braxton, Usher, Janet Babyface to "Drunk in love" by Beyonce. You name them.

The mood was set for the night. He whispered lush words into her ears as he stroke her hair gently.

"I love you Stacy, your amazing qualities are inexhaustible, I would choose you again and again, a thousands times over. You're gorgeous, sweet, funny. Where have you been all my life, Stacy? Where?

(Blushes deeply), She felt like the only woman in the world.

My God! This guy had skills. It'd literally be impossible for one not to succumb to this enticing atmosphere.

"Don't be silly, she said in between a giggle.

Her hand tingled where he held her; he pulled her close to him and kissed her, then, again and again. They had a sexual experience greater than your wildest dreams. The rest is history. All she could think about afterward was him, his touch, caresses, his warmth. She became obsessed with the desire to be with him always, and Marco never let her starve of his presence. He had her hooked on to him. She thought she had loved before, but this right here was an experience she'd never had.

Their relationship progressed and became rather serious. Marco could confess that he'd never been so engrossed with anyone else before Stacy. There was something about her that kept making him come back. Conversations began to come up about Stacy meeting Marco's family. She was particularly excited about this part, though nervous. This was her first "real" relationship, and this move right here was a step further into settling properly with him.

CHAPTER TWO

WHEN IT BEGINS TO UNVEIL

It's was 9 p.m; they'd just had an amazing night date together. Marco drove Stacy to his house so she could meet his mom. He had pre-informed his mother about her coming and expected that his mom was prepared to meet his girlfriend: the person who had been driving him crazy lately.

Stacy was shy and didn't know what she was going to do or say, so she walked closely behind Marco, whose figure kept her hidden conveniently.

"It's about time you got home, Marco's mom said.

Marco kept using signals to let her know he was with someone (his girlfriend), and she needed to put on clothes. Yes, you guessed right, she was naked!

Stacy was completely astonished and didn't know how to react. This situation was really awkward for her, and she just stood still, holding onto Marco.

"Oh, sorry dear, Marco's mom said as she grabbed a piece

of clothing to cover herself, her facials clearly revealed that she acted as though Marco weren't present.

Why was she naked, though? Marco's mother was well aware she was meeting with Stacy tonight and deliberately waited without clothes on. A red flag Stacy should have taken note of, but she was too naive to see it as anything.

Months passed, Marco and Stacy remained together; this was not something Marco's mom was used to. Usually, he never dated a girl for more than a month or two. She thought Stacy must have had a strong influence on him to have remained this long. Was her son falling in love with this beautiful young damsel?

It was never in her character to allow ladies hang around her son for too long. To her, no one was good enough for him. She began to unleash trouble for both of them.

Marco loved to spend his time with Stacy; whenever he wasn't working, Stacy was beside him. His mom knew this and wasn't comfortable; she would keep calling his phone anytime she didn't see him till he came home. Trying to keep the peace, Marco never mentioned his mom's attitude to Stacy; he had to come to really like the girl and didn't want their relationship to halt; at the same time, he tried to make his mom lie low.

CHAPTER THREE

FIERY

Things became ugly, Marco's mom was hell-bent on dissolving her son's relationship with Stacy, and she would stop at nothing. Marco, aside from being frustrated, had also become clueless about steps to take going forward. He'd kept his distance from Stacy against his will, though, so his mom wouldn't go physical with her.

Days passed, and Stacy began to perceive something was off with her prince charming. The same guy who bought her flowers every day and took her to nice restaurants to chill barely called her now. The more she tried to reach him, the more he fended off communication with her. She couldn't contain the pain and hurt she was going through and decided to keep her distance as well. Maybe, just maybe, she'd find a way of forgetting about him eventually.

On the other hand, Marco couldn't take his mind off her; he had fallen head over heels for this lady and wanted to be with no one else but her. The situation with his mom was silently taking him down, and he couldn't take it anymore; he'd begun to stalk her. Everywhere she went, he followed.

She decided to ease up on him so their relationship could continue. Maybe she was too hard on him after all. Marco was completely not the person she'd known. He'd put up a lot of strange attitude recently on countless occasions, and it got Stacy worried. They didn't get to see each other as often as they usually did, and on the days they saw each other, he was either intoxicated on alcohol, weed or acted in very aggressive ways. He wouldn't let her into his home anymore but preferred they see each other at her place. He wanted attention whenever he desired it but wasn't willing to give his attention when it was the other way round. More disturbing, if there was anything they did at ease now, it was to fight.

He gave her a lot of reasons that she'd begun to question if he still wanted the relationship or not. He became toxic and dangerous; this part Stacy didn't know how to handle. She once again kept her distance.

CHAPTER FOUR

MELTDOWN

One particular night, he kept banging hard on the door; the whole neighborhood was disturbed; this compelled her to let him in, so attention was not drawn to them. At least, this time around, she hoped they'd have a chat, and she'd find out what exactly it is that was going on. It'd been over a week now since they last saw each other; he looked tattered, almost like he had not eaten, slept, or had a good bath in days.

There was an awkward silence between them for minutes. He kept staring into her face and tapping his feet. There seemed to be so much rage in him that he needed to take deep breaths and be calm.

"Marco, ain't you gonna talk? You've been staring at me for over 20 minutes; what's wrong, what's going on?

He looked away from her and bowed his head.

"Marco! she yelled.

He had a panic attack, ran out of the living room into the kitchen and put his hand over the flames of the burner, and began to cry and scream, "I can't take it anymore, I can't take it...."

Stacy was scared to death and didn't know what to do. Marco didn't listen to her plea to take his hands off and be calm. She picked up her phone and called the police.

"Marco, I still love you, come on, please don't do this to yourself, please, Stacy pleaded amidst tears.

He'd taken his hands off the fire after a fleeting glance at her face and sat on the floor. His hands had got charred to a certain degree and needed urgent medical attention. Stacy was trying to wrap her mind around what had happened when the policemen knocked on her door.

Ma'am, are you okay? One of the officers asked.

Yes...I am, but he isn't; he's hurting himself. Stacy said, pointing toward Marco, who sat like a toddler on the ground.

The officers wondered why a grown-up in his thirties was seated on the floor, all soaked in tears.

Sir, is everything okay?" the officers asked.

I want to die, Marco answered. I want to die, I love her, I want to be with her, but my mom won't let me. Why won't she let me? I don't wanna live if she ain't with me officers.

Stacy now realized what this whole episode was all about.

All the while, he didn't seem to know how to handle the situation with his mom and so became distant and aggressive.

"Marco, but why didn't you tell me this?"

Need it to be said that he never wanted her to feel bad about the fact that his mom didn't approve of their relationship?

The officers, however, knew at that moment that Marco needed to check his mental health before his condition deteriorated. This they did as they ushered him out.

Stacy figured Marco's mom was a psychopath, but she wasn't going to leave the love of her life either, not now, not while he was seeking help. She'd gotten in touch with a therapist in town who Marco would occasionally visit and talk to. Somehow, he wasn't so open to Stacy as regards all that he was facing with her. It was obvious however, that he'd gone through depression and needed help to work through the problems he'd had.

At first, Marco was reluctant to seek help, but Stacy was there to encourage him that it was necessary for him to be given therapy. They both eventually found a way to stay together, ready to face whatever came now.

Nevertheless, his mom was also not going to give up either; she would go to any length to see to it that she got rid of this lady that had come to share her son with her.

Okay, I don't get this; one would expect that a mother is happy that her son has seen someone he'd love to marry. But this was not the case with Marco's mom.

Alright…Time to break the ice…

Marco and his mother were involved in a sexual relationship for many years now, and it didn't look like it was ending anytime soon.

Surprised? These things happen. Marco spending time with other ladies meant less time with her, and she didn't want that. Keeping him away from others also meant protecting their dirty little secret and that she'd go to any length to do. At this stage, Marco couldn't stand up to his mom to say 'no' anytime she came to sleep with him.

She'd begun this for as long as he can remember. Before he matured, he thought it was a normal thing mothers did to their children, especially sons. Of course, those were the mindless lies his mom told him. He had no idea then that his mom only molested him at every chance she got. She couldn't explain why she was attracted to her son that way, and even when her family found out, she didn't feel any shame or embarrassment; rather, she continued. Her family thought that she probably missed her husband's presence around her and advised her severally to remarry, but she chose to remain that way.

Since Marco's dad died, it'd just being the two of them, and the tie became stronger than what it usually was. Before he even became a teenager, his mom had exposed him to a lot more than he should have been exposed to. Though he began dating quite early, he'd never let his mom know he had a girlfriend till he was a bit older. The first time his mom saw him with a girl, he was in his first year in junior high school; she'd aggressively sent her away from the house and warned him sternly never to bring a girl home.

When Marco was all grown up, he began bringing some ladies he dated home. All of those he dated before now couldn't stand his mom the very moment she began brewing trouble for them, they left.. She'd controlled him all his life that even when he'd got a good job and could live on his own, she refused. One could only wonder how manipulative she was. Well, at this rate, one should easily think that Marco wasn't really her child.

CHAPTER FIVE

NEVER IGNORE THE RED FLAGS

At this time, Stacy was already expecting his baby. When she got to know she was pregnant, she wasn't so excited but hoped the news of her expecting a baby would bond them. But he only felt obligated to put a ring on her finger, a ploy to keep her tied down while he and his mom continued their charade. He was never going to marry her; he just wanted a child, nothing more.

Her pregnancy was getting further along, and his mom was hell-bent on sabotaging their relationship. Stacy doubted countless times if she wanted to continue holding onto this relationship with Marco, but the pregnancy now was something she needed to really consider for whatever decision she was going to make.

Marco's mom found her son another lover to occupy his time so much that he didn't have time for Stacy anymore.

"The only thing you can give my son that I can't is a baby, she'd say to Stacy.

His mom's viciousness and cruelty towards her were tormenting. She couldn't believe most times that the "calm" woman she met six months ago was a narcissistic witch and a terrible one at that. There was no night she didn't go to bed feeling uneasy about the circumstances that surrounded her or the thorn-like thoughts as to what she had done to deserve such hate. How was she going to handle both her boyfriend and his mother? She really loved Marco, and she didn't want to have to leave him because of his mom.

One day after work, Stacy returned to see her apartment in a shambles; Marco's mom had just wrecked the whole place. She got so mad, pacing about, breathing hard, trying to use up her anger but couldn't help but flare. This time, she couldn't stomach this without giving Marco's mom a piece of her mind. Straight away, she headed for his mom's house and began to pour out all that she'd bottled up on her inside. She'd hardly been in this fit of rage all her life.

His mom didn't stop, Marco wasn't ever there to defend her either. How would he? He alone was enough trouble for her. Stacy fell into depression the days that followed, the office worked piled, and she had to look after herself alone. She was clueless about how to take care of her pregnancy, and everything had gone so near to hell in this experience that six months ago, she didn't know she'd be at this point she was now.

Fast forward to two weeks later, Stacy got worse; she was in severe pain emotionally and mentally. Marco barely had time for her now, when they saw each other, he'd apologize for all that was happening, try to convince her he loved her, and then go back to doing the same things he'd just apologized about.

Well, you know how there are certain junctures you get to in life that you begin to wonder how you'll survive them? That was where she'd found herself now.

While he spent more time with the other lady, his mom set him up with who was beginning to fall for him already, she'd threatened the more to take away Stacy's child once she delivers him. She faced humiliation and abuse every day that passed but didn't know where to get help. Her mind would wander back to the first time they met at the store, he was such a lovely and handsome gentleman. Though she liked him almost immediately, she had to play hard to get for a while before giving into Marco's persistent wooing.

She'd just become independent of her family; crossing paths with Marco made her feel she had met the ideal husband and was ready to settle down. All of that was now a mirage, and to top it off, she was pregnant.

I believe it's quite difficult to admit you're in an abusive relationship, especially when all seemed rosy from the beginning.

CHAPTER SIX

CONSEQUENCES IN LIFE

Marco's side chick became obsessed with him. She couldn't stand the fact that he had another woman in his life and began to scheme how to get rid of her. Marco's mom sure didn't see this coming, and of course, the outcome would be a disaster class.

One morning, Stacy had just settled in her office when Marco's side chick walked in.

"Don't you know how to knock?" Stacy asked, irritated by the way she barged in.

"Well, I'm not here to be nice", she answered with a look of disdain on her face. "I'm here to force it down your throat that I'm dating your man.

At that instant, silence prevailed within Stacy. Of course, the silence that saved the day. Marco's side chick was disappointed she didn't get the reaction she expected.

"Well, uh... aren't you gonna say anything to me. I'd manage to hear you out?"

At this point, Stacy had had enough of the crazy drama between Marco and his mom; she wanted out. Besides, he was the least of her worries.

"Hey, hey, I said I am dating your man, and quite frankly, I don't want you interrupting our lives.

"You know what, you can have him all to yourself for all I care, Stacy said, dropping the pen between her thumb and index finger.

There were so many red flags she had seen over time that she wasn't gonna ignore anymore, and even if it meant raising her kid on her own, she was ready to do that away from the craziness of Marco and his mom.

It wasn't just the putting his hands on a flaming burner or the sleeping with his mom thing. Yes she knew about that now, his grandparents had called her aside one day and told her, he had once attempted suicide with an overdose of pills. Another time, he almost killed both of them on a cliff because he thought they were going to be separated. What more hell with this crazy side chick? Hell no!!!

Marco's side chick was mad that her exposing the relationship she had with Marco to Stacy didn't bother her, she stormed out of the office angrily and headed for her apartment. If she wasn't going to have him, then no one was. She searched her room inside out for her gun. Everywhere was littered with her stuff till she could locate it somewhere under her bed.

Marco stopped over at Stacy's office to pick her up, and his side chick knew exactly what time he'd come. As Stacy walked out the door with Marco, she fired the gun, aiming directly at his chest and then took off. Marco fell to the ground, his hand pressing against the wounded area as he screamed in anguish. Stacy joined him, screaming for help as she tried to also stop the bleeding. Her efforts didn't seem to be helping; she picked up her phone to call his mom.

"Somebody call an ambulance, shouted a lady amongst the people that were already gathering around.

Marco was helpless, the pool he found himself enmeshed in (blood of course), he knew he wasn't going to survive. He began to plead for Stacy's forgiveness with tears trickling.

Stacy couldn't help it, she began to weep too. His mom hurried to the scene but met her son already given up the ghost. She couldn't contain herself, she went haywire. Her only son, her precious boy was dying and she couldn't save him. Before the ambulance arrived, Marco had died. The two women sat beside the newly-dead with a handful of sympathizers and onlookers surrounding them.

Marco's mom realized what a mess she was, she began to question her actions. When did she become this monster she was? Why did she treat her son the way she did? Why was she so controlling? He could have lived his life happy with whoever he wanted, but she'd turned him to her toy. Her plot to keep Marco all to herself led to his demise in the end, all she could do now was bow her head in regret.

It was a Saturday morning, three days after Marco's death, his family had gathered to give him last respects and commit his body to earth. Stacy could not help but be emotional. Somehow, even with the latest drama that played out, she still loved her man.

Rites followed on, but all she could think of was the memories she had with Marco.

"There's a time appointed for everything under heaven", the Pastor read on; "a time to be born and a time to die....."

"Not this way, not like this, not now, when I'm still pregnant with his baby", Stacy sobbed in silent agony.

After the funeral, she walked up to Marco's mom.

"I'm sorry that I ever came between you and your son, we both know that things didn't have to end this way" she said as she walked out.

On her way home, she resolved she was going to live her life drama-free, the crazy episode had finally come to an end though tragically. If there was anything she'd learned from the toxic relationship, it was to never ever ignore the "Red flags".

This behavior isn't just affecting Daughters and Fathers… Mental illness is real, it stems from stories such as these. Seek help to break the GENERATIONAL CURSES.

THE END

ABOUT THE AUTHOR

Debbie"Saffron" Stevens believes in leading and not following unless she's gaining knowledge, wisdom and guidance to help deliver empowerment to women becoming free from bondage to live a life of peace. Allowing the untold and shameful stories that no one wants to talk about because of it's embarrassment and humiliation to come to life. If her Collections reaches only one person and she becomes FREE that's what this is all for (reach one teach one).

Debbie 'Saffron' Stevens is a very humble woman of God". She herself has been through a total METAMORPHOSIS in her lifetime; from the cocoon to a Total BUTTERFLY she considers  herself FREE.

Very loving mother of three: Ebonee (Nieko) Stevens; Londyn Je'nee Stevens; Antonyo (Tony) Stevens; Ronnie Williams (My son by another mother)

And the Very proud Glam Ma to Princess Melrose (Mellie) born to my (first born Ebonee Nieko Stevens) the year of Covid 19" 2020. (GOD gave us a total Blessing)!

*more "Saffron MindBenders Collections" to come...

www.ingramcontent.com/pod-product-compliance
Lightning Source LLC
Chambersburg PA
CBHW060947130726
48001CB00003B/1095